D1032752

Football

by Ray McClellan

BELLWETHER MEDIA • MINNEAPOLIS, MN

BLASTOFF!
4
READERS

Note to Librarians, Teachers, and Parents:

Blastoff! Readers are carefully developed by literacy experts and combine standards-based content with developmentally appropriate text.

Level 1 provides the most support through repetition of high-frequency words, light text, predictable sentence patterns, and strong visual support.

Level 2 offers early readers a bit more challenge through varied simple sentences, increased text load, and less repetition of high-frequency words.

Level 3 advances early-fluent readers toward fluency through increased text and concept load, less reliance on visuals, longer sentences, and more literary language.

Level 4 builds reading stamina by providing more text per page, increased use of punctuation, greater variation in sentence patterns, and increasingly challenging vocabulary.

Level 5 encourages children to move from "learning to read" to "reading to learn" by providing even more text, varied writing styles, and less familiar topics.

Whichever book is right for your reader, Blastoff! Readers are the perfect books to build confidence and encourage a love of reading that will last a lifetime!

This edition first published in 2010 by Bellwether Media, Inc.

No part of this publication may be reproduced in whole or in part without written permission of the publisher. For information regarding permission, write to Bellwether Media, Inc., Attention: Permissions Department, Post Office Box 19349, Minneapolis, MN 55419.

Library of Congress Cataloging-in-Publication Data
McClellan, Ray.
  Football / by Ray McClellan.
    p. cm. – (Blastoff! readers. My first sports)
  Includes bibliographical references and index.
  Summary: "Simple text and full color photographs introduce beginning readers to the sport of football. Developed by literacy experts for students in grades two through five"–Provided by publisher.
    ISBN 978-1-60014-194-2 (hardcover : alk. paper)
  1. Football–Juvenile literature. I. Title.

GV950.7.M33 2009
796.332–dc22
                              2009008187

Contents

What Is Football?

Football is a team sport most popular in the United States. Kids, adults, and professionals around the world enjoy the game. The American game of football has existed for almost 150 years.

rugby

Football grew out of the sports of rugby and soccer. Walter Camp invented American football in the 1870s. He got the idea for the sport when he saw someone pick up a soccer ball and run with it.

The National Football League (NFL) started in the early 1920s. The American Football League (AFL) started in 1960. In 1967, the first **Super Bowl** was played. The AFL became a part of the NFL in 1970.

The Basic Rules of Football

quarterback

The goal in football is to move the ball and score points. The **offense** must move the ball ten yards forward within four plays, or downs, to get a **first down**.

The **quarterback** leads the offense. This player can run the ball or hand the ball off to a runner. They can also throw the ball to a player down the field.

fun fact

The line of scrimmage is where each play begins.

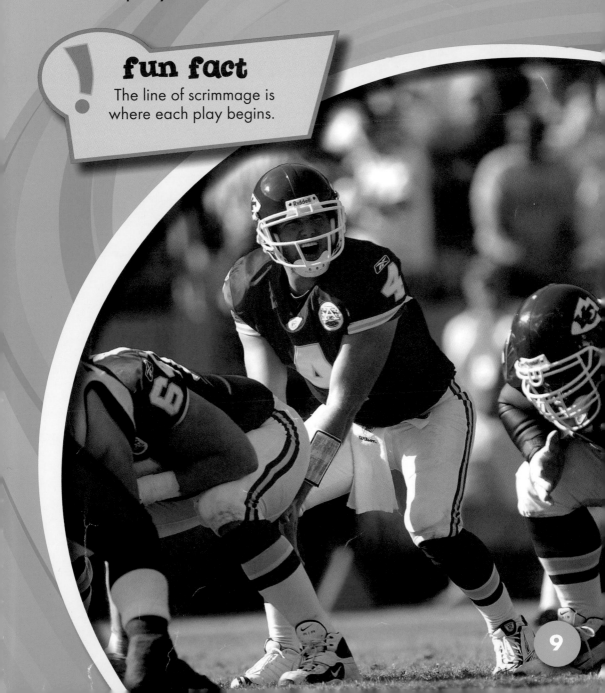

The offense can score points in different ways.
They can score a three-point **field goal** by
kicking the ball through the **goal posts**.
They can score a six-point **touchdown** by
getting the ball into the opponent's **end zone**.

After a touchdown, a team can kick the ball through the goal posts for an extra point or try for a **two-point conversion**.

fun fact

In most of the world, the word "football" refers to the sport Americans call soccer. People use the term "American football" to describe the game.

The **defense** tries to stop the ball carrier. When the ball carrier is stopped, the play is over. The defense can get control of the ball by recovering a **fumble** or making an **interception**.

They can also force the offense to **punt**.
The defense can score a two-point **safety**
by tackling the offensive ball carrier in the
offense's end zone.

Football Equipment

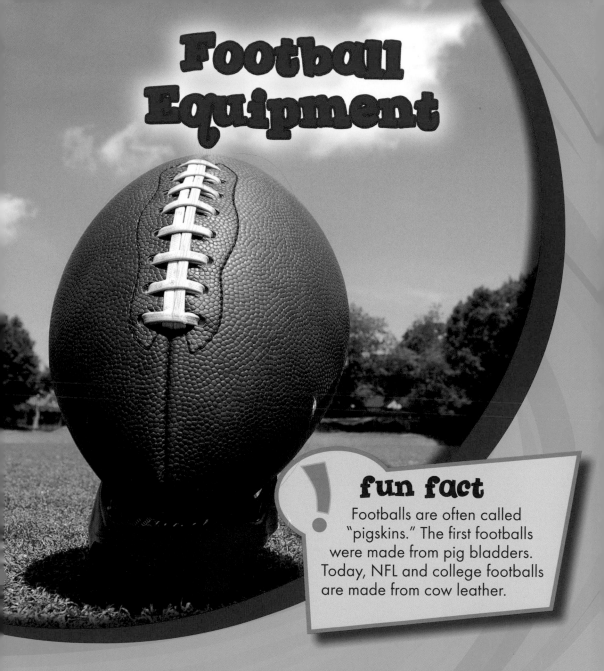

fun fact

Footballs are often called "pigskins." The first footballs were made from pig bladders. Today, NFL and college footballs are made from cow leather.

The football is the most important piece of equipment in the game. A football has an oval shape.

It is made of leather with white laces for gripping. An official NFL football weighs about 15 ounces (425 grams).

Football is a hard-hitting game. Players need helmets with face masks. Mouth guards protect players' teeth. Players need strong pads on their shoulders, chests, and legs.

For games on grass fields, players wear
shoes with **cleats**. These spikes on the
bottom of the shoes dig into the ground
and provide grip.

Football Today

Peyton Manning

Football is very popular today in the United States and Canada. From games in the backyard to high school to the NFL, people of all ages love to play and watch the sport.

Adrian Peterson

Stars such as Peyton Manning, Adrian Peterson, and Tom Brady lead the way.

The NFL has 32 teams split into two conferences that are each made up of four divisions.

Six teams from each conference make the play-offs. The two conference champions meet in the Super Bowl. Fans love to watch players run, throw, and kick their way to victory.

Glossary

cleats—the metal spikes attached to the soles of shoes to provide grip on grass fields

defense—the team trying to stop the offense from scoring

end zone—the scoring zone at either end of a football field; an offense must move the ball into an opponent's end zone to score a touchdown.

field goal—a three-point score earned by kicking the ball through the goal posts

first down—when the offense moves the ball ten yards forward in four plays or fewer

fumble—when the ball carrier drops the ball before being tackled; either team can pick up the loose ball.

goal posts—a set of posts placed at the back of each end zone

interception—a play in which a defensive player catches a forward pass, giving the defense the ball

offense—the team trying to score; a team on offense has the ball.

punt—to kick the ball away after a team fails to earn a first down

quarterback—the offensive player who takes the ball to begin each play; the quarterback can hand the ball off to a runner, run himself, or throw the ball to a player down the field.

safety—a two-point score made when the defense tackles the offensive ball carrier in the offense's end zone

Super Bowl—the championship game of the NFL

touchdown—a six-point score earned by carrying the ball into the end zone or catching the ball in the end zone

two-point conversion—a play after a touchdown in which the offense has one chance to move the ball into the end zone for two points

To Learn More

AT THE LIBRARY

Buckman, Virginia. *Football Stars*. New York, N.Y.: Children's Press, 2007.

Dougherty, Terri. *The Greatest Football Records*. Mankato, Minn.: Capstone, 2009.

Gigliotti, Jim. *Football*. Ann Arbor, Mich.: Cherry Lake, 2009.

ON THE WEB

Learning more about football is as easy as 1, 2, 3.

1. Go to www.factsurfer.com.

2. Enter "football" into the search box.

3. Click the "Surf" button and you will see a list of related Web sites.

With factsurfer.com, finding more information is just a click away.

Index

The images in this book are reproduced through the courtesy of: James Boulette, front cover; Mikeljay, pp. 4-5; Marty Melville / Stringer / Getty Images, p. 6; Focus on Sports / Getty Images, p. 7; David Drapkin, pp. 8, 20, 21; G. Newman Lowrance, p. 9; Jerry Sharp, p. 10; Iris Nieves, p. 11; Dennis MacDonald / Age Fotostock, p. 12; Steve Dykes / Getty Images, p. 13; Chris Scredon, p. 14; Ronald Martinez, p. 15; GPI Stock / Alamy, p. 16; Paul Spinelli / Getty Images, p. 17; Sam Greenwood / Getty Images, p. 18; Tom Dahlin / Getty Images, p. 19.